You Drive like an
ASSHOLE

*And Your Parking Sucks, Too!

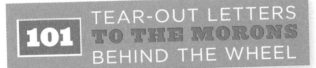

101 TEAR-OUT LETTERS
TO THE MORONS
BEHIND THE WHEEL

TOMMY BLACHA

RUNNING PRESS
PHILADELPHIA · LONDON

Books published by Running Press are available at special discounts for
bulk purchases in the United States by corporations, institutions, and
other organizations. For more information, please contact the Special
Markets Department at the Perseus Books Group, 2300 Chestnut Street,
Suite 200, Philadelphia, PA 19103, or call (800) 810-4145, ext. 5000, or
e-mail special.markets@perseusbooks.com.

ISBN 978-0-7624-5867-7
Library of Congress Control Number: 2015934576

E-book ISBN 978-0-7624-5883-7

9   8   7   6   5   4   3   2   1
Digit on the right indicates the number of this printing

Cover and interior design by Melissa Gerber
Edited by Jordana Tusman
Typography: 2011 Slimtype Sans Italic, Andalusia Regular, Avenir Book,
Avenir Book Oblique, Comic Sans MS PS Regular, Emmascript MVB, GFY
Brutus, GFY Hey Steve, GFY Jacks Blueprint, GFY Jeanna, GFY Mancini,
GFY Peggy, GFY Pollak, GFY Shue, GFY Sidney, GFY Sonya, Gotham,
Grimsby Hand, Gros Marqueur, Rough LT Medium Italic, Times New
Roman PS MT Roman, Tully Light, and Ziggurat Black.

Running Press Book Publishers
2300 Chestnut Street
Philadelphia, PA 19103-4371

Visit us on the web!
www.runningpress.com

CONTENTS

Working Vehicles

Pool Maintenance Idiots, Lawn-Care Morons, Garbage Trucks, and Construction Vehicles

Shitty-Car Owners

They're the Owners of the Shittiest Cars on the Road—Does That Also Mean They Have to Be the Shittiest Drivers?

Texters and Phone Users

Not Just Limited to Asshole Teenagers

RVs, Boat Trailers, and Snowmobile Haulers

Insufferable Assholes Who Are Having Way More Fun Than You

Vanity-Plate Assholes
Personal Vanity Plates and the Assholes Who Obtain Them

Car Decorators
Special Idiots Who Have to Flaunt Their Religious and Political Affiliations on Their Bumpers

Tourists and Fans
Assholes Who Like to Look Around in Amazement While Driving

Everyday Assholes
Regular, Everyday Assholes— Could Even Be You or Me!

Dear Asshole Reading
This Introduction,

There are almost a billion cars on the road at any given moment. That means our beautiful earth is infested with hundreds of millions of assholes making mind-bogglingly stupid choices with their big, dumb, stupid cars every second of every day. And the number is growing—which is far more terrifying than anything a science-fiction movie could ever conjure up. How many asshole drivers on the road do you see daily? At least five, sometimes five hundred?

Use the tear-out letters in this book to express your displeasure with the madness we see every day on our roads. Don't let these metal machines rob our human souls of everything good and decent. Stop your pointless swearing and steering-wheel pounding. Stop your openmouthed, astonished gaze. Stop muttering to yourself, and do something about it! Slap these letters on the wrongdoers' windshields (making sure no one sees you do it, of course), and shout to the heavens: "My God! You drive like an ASSHOLE!"

Sincerely,
The Folks at You Drive Like an Asshole

Dear Asshole in the Gorgeous, White,
Mercedes S-Class,

Hello!? CAN YOU HEAR ME? I know you have sealed
yourself off with your tinted windows and air-conditioning.
Sorry for bothering you, my perfumed princess. I am just
one of the lowly subhumans that you occasionally run off
the road. It must be hard to pay attention to the road with
all of your luxury devices and plush, white leather seats. I
would like to respectfully remind Your Royal Highness that
there are actual people driving in the vehicles you constantly
force off the road. If I could have just one moment of your
time and give you a message from the common folk, it is as
follows: "You stuck up, unaware, horrifying, VAPID, SELF-
ABSORBED, PLASTIC SURGERY DISASTER!
You are driving like an ASSHOLE!"

Regards,

_____

Dear Asshole in the
Gorgeous, White,
Mercedes S-Class

DEAR ASSHOLE TOO YOUNG TO AFFORD THAT CAR,

MAYBE YOU ARE SLIDING AROUND ON A PHONE BOOK BECAUSE YOU ARE TOO SMALL AND YOUNG TO REACH THE PEDALS. MAYBE YOU DON'T KNOW WHAT A PHONE BOOK IS BECAUSE YOU WERE BORN LAST THURSDAY. MAYBE YOU THINK YOU ARE PLAYING A VIDEO GAME AND THIS ISN'T REAL LIFE. MAYBE YOU HAVE SMOKED YOUR FIRST JOINT AND ARE TOO HIGH. MAYBE YOU ARE HOPPED UP ON SUGARY CEREAL.

SURE, I HAVE SOME RESENTMENT BECAUSE YOUR CAR IS WORTH MORE THAN EVERYTHING MY FATHER EARNED IN HIS WHOLE LIFE WHILE YOU CAN'T EVEN SHAVE YET, AND YOUR VOICE IS PROBABLY STILL CHANGING. BUT THAT DOESN'T CHANGE THE FACT THAT, REGARDLESS OF YOUR AGE, YOU ARE A DIM-WITTED DUMB FUCK, WHO WILL HOPEFULLY WIND UP OVERTURNED IN SOME OLD PEOPLE'S FRONT YARD, AND THEY WILL COME OUT AND BEAT YOU TO DEATH WITH THEIR CANES. YOU—WITH YOUR WEAK LITTLE HANDS, AND YOUR STUPID BABY FEET— DRIVE LIKE AN ASSHOLE!

SINCERELY,

_____

DEAR ASSHOLE TOO YOUNG
TO AFFORD THAT CAR

Dear Good-Looking Asshole in the Italian Sports Car,

Your car is not a time machine. It is not 1961. You are not Marcello Mastroianni. You are not sophisticated, urbane, or even European. Your romantic exploits are not interesting. Your "art" is not lasting. Your engine does not make up for the defects in your character. You are an overly gelled, overly manicured douche bag, swerving in and out of lanes with the top down on a 58-degree day. The most romantic thing you could do would be to wrap that car around a telephone pole. You drive like an asshole.

Ciao,

_____

Dear Good-Looking Asshole
in the Italian Sports Car

Dear Ugly Asshole in the Italian Sports Car,

Wow! You sure are ugly! That fancy car isn't working for you. It must be hard to watch the road when you keep glancing at yourself in the mirror and see a monster driving that nice car. Doesn't quite seem to fit, does it? Did you ever peek out from under those designer sunglasses to catch a glimpse of those pig eyes? Now glance in the sideview mirror to see if anyone is in the lane next to you. Damn! There you are again! So dumb-looking in that nice car. Oops! I guess you cut someone off again. I guess you just want people to see your blurred face as it goes whizzing by. I'm sorry. You can't outrun your dumb, ugly face. Either get a new mug or a car that fits, because that car is making you drive like an asshole!

Not Admiringly,

_____

Dear Ugly Asshole
in the Italian Sports Car

Dear Eastern European
Mobster Asshole,

Hey, Boris. I don't know how things
are in Jerkistan, Kadzookiestan, or
Moscow, but even if you have a note
from Vladimir Putin himself, you
aren't allowed to drive any way you
want in this country. Of course,
I'll never actually glare right at
you, because you seem terrifying—
I'm sure you've killed people, and you
look like your nose has been broken
a hundred times. If I had more
guts, I'd slash your tires or break
your window, but I've summoned up
enough courage to leave this letter
on your windshield to let you know
that you drive like a fucking asshole.

Proudly, Americanly yours,

Dear Eastern European
Mobster Asshole

Dear Urban Asshole with the Monster SUV,

Do you live in that thing? Where do you park it? Why do you need that huge truck in the city? There is no need for you to be insecure. Your stupid face would still look really stupid, even if you were on a skateboard. Believe me. Everyone knows what a fuckface you are, no matter what you are driving. You just have one of those faces. I will admit that it is enhanced by your ridiculous monster perch. Look, if there were boulders in the middle of these streets, I would understand your need for that vehicle. But you are not crushing buses in an arena somewhere. You are simply driving around the city, cutting people off because you can't properly see them ten feet below you. I must decree that YOU drive like an asshole!!

Hatefully yours,

_____

Dear Urban Asshole
with the Monster SUV

Dear Rural Asshole with the Monster SUV,

I get it. Back roads! Open spaces! Huge pickup truck! It all makes sense. Except, you are not hauling anything massive! You are not driving over anything at this exact moment, so therefore, you look like a moron. Don't you spend 98 percent of your income on gas? Every person in a three-county radius has dents from your mongo tires spitting gravel at them. You should get a trucker hat that says, "I have a small, miserable penis." It would look good over your constantly open, heavy-breathing mouth and gnarled dog teeth. The rows of corn and tree stumps are mighty impressed with you, but even they realize that you drive like an asshole!

Good-bye, Turd,

_____

Dear Rural Asshole
with the Monster SUV

Dear Beloved-Senior-Citizen Asshole,

I really do appreciate the fact that you've been on this planet for so many decades, but there comes a time when we have to realize we can't do some things like we used to, like, oh, maybe . . . SEE! . . . OR THINK! Pardon me, but your crabby, old, shitty face and your extremely slow driving are detriments to everyone else on the road. Please pull over in the next graveyard and simply expire. That is how shitty your driving is. You drive like an asshole.

With respect,

_____

P.S. Please don't park somewhere secluded and die in your car. Some young person might want to buy it.

Dear Beloved-Senior-
Citizen Asshole

Dear Classic-Car-Driving Asshole,

You did it! You finally saved up enough money for your classic car. How come everyone who drives these cars looks just like you? White hair, Hawaiian shirt, stupid shorts, red, sunburned face. Your car looks very clean and highly shiny. It's obvious your life is over except for your classic car. It's clear that you drive from one classic car show to another going exactly TEN MILES AN HOUR!!! You don't have long, as you'll be having a massive heart attack within the next year, but in the meantime, could you kindly drive a little faster? Because you're driving like an asshole.

Youthfully yours,

_____

Dear Classic-Car-Driving Asshole

Dear 1970s-Muscle-Car-Driving Asshole,

Holy shit, listen to that engine! Look at those big, fat tires! Here's the thing though: You're driving on fucking side streets, you fucking idiot! I love your impressive forty-yard bursts of speed before you have to stop for the stop sign and then your next forty-yard burst of speed before you have to stop for a red light. Have you seen the end of *Thelma & Louise*? It's a movie from the '90s that has a really good ending. I think you should watch it. There are actually a lot of good car movies from the '70s in which the hero drives into a train and/or a brick wall. Just something to think about next time you're behind the wheel, and you realize that forty yards of side-street racing is not enough to satisfy you. Your car looks cool, but your head looks stupid in it. You drive like an asshole.

Patiently awaiting your demise,

_____

Dear 1970s-Muscle-Car-
Driving Asshole

RUSH HOUR!

The Crème de la Crème of Assholes

Dear Makeup-Applying Asshole,

Are you extremely late and about to be on live TV? Are you going to drive up, screech to a halt, rush out of your car, and immediately be on camera? If not, why do you feel it is absolutely necessary to apply lipstick and eye shadow when you pull up to every stop—and even while you're driving? Is it that important? Are you that hideous without makeup? Couldn't you stop and wait to apply it half a block from wherever the fuck it is you're going? I hope you get rear-ended and your lipstick goes up your nose, destroying the portion of your brain that makes you want to put makeup on. You drive like a fucking asshole.

Pleasantly,

_____

P.S. Forget the makeup and spring for a face-lift. But not while driving!

Dear Makeup-Applying Asshole

DEAR ZIT-POPPING-IN-THE-REARVIEW-MIRROR ASSHOLE,

OH MY GOD, WHAT ARE YOU DOING? ARE YOU POPPING A ZIT IN THE MIRROR? GROSS! CAN'T YOU JUST WAIT UNTIL YOU STOP TO DO THAT? DO YOU HAVE TO GET THE PUS OUT OF THAT ZIT RIGHT NOW, WHILE YOU'RE DRIVING? WILL SPIDER EGGS HATCH OUT OF YOUR FACE? DO ME A FAVOR AND AT LEAST WAIT UNTIL A RED LIGHT TO POP THAT ZIT, BECAUSE THERE IS NO POSSIBLE WAY TO LOOK IN YOUR REARVIEW MIRROR, STEER, POP A ZIT, AND NOT DRIVE LIKE A COMPLETE FUCKING ASSHOLE ALL AT THE SAME TIME.

YOUR ACNE-FREE FELLOW MOTORIST,

_____

DEAR ZIT-POPPING-
IN-THE-REARVIEW-
MIRROR ASSHOLE

Dear Obsessive-Lane-Changing Asshole,

For fuck's sake, stay in one lane, you complete piece of shit. Yes, I know, some lanes move faster than others. Occasionally, we go in and out of them, but not every two fucking seconds! I don't see a pregnant woman's water breaking in your car or a gunshot victim in your backseat. You don't look like Bruce Willis in *Die Hard* on the way to save us from some terrorists. Therefore, I repeat: Stay in one lane, you annoying, pinball fuckhead of a driver. You drive like an asshole.

Frustratingly yours,

_____

Dear Obsessive-Lane-Changing Asshole

Dear Rush-Hour-Taxi-Driving Asshole,

The question is, "Were you born this way, or did driving a cab in rush hour make you this way?" According to some theories, your car exhaust is going into the driver's seat, but one thing everyone agrees on is that you drive like a true psychopath! Don't the voices in your head ever yell, "SLOW DOWN, YOU FUCKING MANIAC!"? I hope every fungal infection, disease, and smell from every person you have ever picked up rises from the backseat and attacks you all at once, and you are forced to drive around the seventh circle of hell for all eternity. Oh, and I hope every fare you pick up is a demon that eats your skin. You drive like an asshole.

Fondly,

_____

P.S. Next time you pick up a fare at the mental hospital, maybe you could pop in for a checkup.

Dear Rush-Hour-
Taxi-Driving Asshole

Dear Frantic, Wet-Haired, Despair-Faced Asshole,

Hey, I get it—you're late for work. Guess what? So is everyone else on this fucking road! If you're that panicked you're running late, why did you insist on taking a fucking shower this morning? Do you really think you're ever going to get a promotion when you make it to your desk five seconds before you're tardy, hyperventilating with that stupid, wet hair? Everyone at work probably hates you. I hope you get demoted and bums shit on your parking space, because you drive like an asshole.

Disrespectfully yours,

_____

P.S. I don't want to see you blow-drying your hair while driving. That is NOT a solution.

Dear Frantic, Wet-Haired,
Despair-Faced Asshole

Dear Horn-Blowing Asshole,

I'm sorry you're having a problem with another driver in the immediate vicinity. We've all experienced such frustration, but now is as good a time as any to remind you that your horn is audible to ALL OF US. You're not having a private conversation between you and another driver. Your horn is certainly not an extension of a silent internal monologue of frustration. I can hear it. We can all hear it. Maybe before blowing your horn again, ask yourself a few simple questions:

1) Am I accomplishing anything (beyond showing everyone I'm an asshole) by constantly honking?

2) Might my frustration with the world be better expressed indoors—say, in the confines of a therapist's office, where assholes are commonly granted patience and understanding in exchange for a reasonable insurance copay?

3) How did I become such an asshole? Is this a reversible process?

Oh wait, you're honking at me? Wait, ME?! There's oncoming traffic! I can't fucking turn left now! It's impossible! Stop your fucking honking! You drive like an asshole!

Loudly,

_____

Dear Horn-Blowing Asshole

DEAR HAZARD-LIGHTS ASSHOLE,

WHY ARE YOU JUST SITTING THERE, STARING? WHAT THE FUCK ARE YOU DOING? ARE YOU HAVING A HEART ATTACK? YES, I KNOW THAT HAZARD LIGHTS HAVE MANY FUNCTIONS, BUT THESE FUNCTIONS DO NOT INCLUDE BEING ABLE TO DOUBLE-PARK WHEREVER THE FUCK YOU WANT. WHY THE FUCK DON'T YOU PARK SOMEWHERE ELSE SO THAT EVERYONE ELSE DOESN'T HAVE TO KEEP GOING AROUND YOU? WAIT A SECOND, DO YOU HAVE A DUMMY FROM A WAX MUSEUM IN YOUR CAR? BECAUSE THAT WOULD BE HILARIOUS. BUT NO, NOW I CAN CLEARLY SEE IT'S JUST YOUR STUPID FACE SITTING IN YOUR STUPID CAR. YOU DRIVE LIKE AN ASSHOLE.

SO ANNOYED AND BORED WITH YOUR EXISTENCE,

_____

DEAR HAZARD-LIGHTS ASSHOLE

Dear Asshole Driving Way Too Fast,

How many body parts of cats, dogs, and old people do you have stuck inside your grill, you fucking asshole? Why do you feel the need to drive that fucking fast all the fucking time? My only hope is that you won't see that speed trap up ahead. Hopefully, you're going fast enough to be arrested and put into one of those extreme-driver-retraining programs, where you have to do community service at a hospital, or something. While some people might feel sympathy because you'll be cleaning up rags soaked in bodily fluid, I will be suppressing a sweet, sweet smile. You drive like an asshole.

Till death do us part,

_____

Dear Asshole Driving
Way Too Fast

Dear Asshole Driving Way Too Slow,

Do you ever wonder why it is that every car races past you, and every driver feels the need to give you a dirty look while doing so? Do you ever wonder why? Maybe it's because you're driving so fucking slowly. Has that thought ever struck you? Because this must happen every day. Is the exhaust leaking into your car? Are you from another planet? Maybe you see things in slow motion. You think you're being extra safe, but you're actually causing a dangerous situation with your timid, slow-as-fuck driving. Stop driving like a super-slow asshole, and move the hell out of everyone's way. Nobody likes you! You drive like an asshole!

Drive faster,

_____

Dear Asshole Driving
Way Too Slow

Dear Drives-Like-a-Cop-But-Isn't Asshole,

I love how you swerved around those cars and easily pulled into that spot like you're a cop. Except for one small problem. You're NOT a cop!! Let me guess the reasons you couldn't become a cop. Couldn't pass the psych test? Couldn't pass the physical-fitness test? Can't see well enough? Too stupid? You sure must have a lot of fun driving around pretending to be a cop, because it's obvious you're one of those types who has a lot of cop fantasies when you're behind the wheel. I hope one day you'll be inside a real cop car—in the backseat, in handcuffs, and going to prison—because someone finally turned you in for all the horrifying things that are no doubt on your computer at home. You drive like an asshole.

Over and out, Jerk,

Dear Drives-Like-a-Cop-
But-Isn't Asshole

Dear Third-Car-through-the-Yellow-Light Asshole,

What do you think you're doing?! It's a time-honored tradition that two cars get to turn left on a yellow light. TWO! You make me so angry with your entitled, third-car-left-turn-through-the-yellow ways. I hope the next time you do this a sewage truck hits you. I'm sure it will take a long time for the firefighters to separate you from the excrement, as you are practically identical. You drive like an asshole.

Hope this note finds you well,

_____

Dear Third-Car-
through-the-Yellow-
Light Asshole

GOVERNMENT AND OFFICIAL VEHICLES

Bloated, Blistering Buses and Arrogant Government Vehicles (Including Fire, Rescue, and Police)

Dear Asshole Bus Driver,

Congratulations for letting the absolute smallest amount of power available to you go to your head. You have the privilege of driving a very large vehicle. That's right, your vehicle is larger than every other vehicle on the road. You must think that gives you the right to wildly swing your bloated ozone layer assassin across two lanes of freely moving, downtown traffic. People will certainly yield to you. We know you won't stop—and we don't want to be crushed to death by a massive orange rectangle being driven by a disgruntled city worker. For some reason, it feels like if we don't get out of your way, we will be the ones at fault. So please continue steamrolling my rights and putting your innocent passengers at risk, because you deserve it. You drive like a real asshole.

Power to the people,

_____

Dear Asshole Bus Driver

Dear Asshole Driving a Privately Owned Ambulance,

What the fuck kind of ambulance are you driving? It isn't something owned by the city. What kind of name is that? You look like you're driving a vehicle for some crappy company that's actually run by aliens from some bad '70s sci-fi movie. You are definitely not an official vehicle. Why do I have to pull over for you? I'm sure you're just transferring crabby old assholes from one nursing home to another. Why are you driving so fast? Don't you make more money if they die? What's your rush? Please stop driving like an asshole.

Get off the road,

_____

Dear Asshole
Driving a Privately
Owned Ambulance

Dear Asshole Driving
a Fire Truck,

Holy fuck! I pulled over—what
more do you want? For fuck's
sake, you blasted through that
intersection like you're going to
smash everything in your path.
I don't know how much more on
the side of the road I can get.
You win—we are all terrified by
your insanely loud horn and your
incredibly aggressive driving.
Look, if you were on the way to
my burning house, I would applaud
you, but since presumably you're
not, you're driving like an asshole.

Stay safe,

_____

Dear Asshole Driving
a Fire Truck

DEAR PARKING-ENFORCEMENT ASSHOLE,

CONGRATULATIONS ON YOUR DOMINION OVER THIS BLOCK. THOUGH YOU MAY NOT HAVE THE AUTHORITY OF A COP IN THE REAL WORLD, WE ALL CONSIDER YOU A MINI-COP OF THE NEIGHBORHOOD. WE LIVE IN FEAR OF YOU DURING STREET-CLEANING TIMES AND QUESTIONABLE HOLIDAYS. YOU ARE CAPABLE OF HANDING OUT FINANCIAL SANCTIONS FIRST THING IN THE MORNING THAT RENDER OUR ENTIRE DAY'S EARNINGS NULL AND VOID. BY SIMPLY WADDLING OUT OF YOUR CAR AND WRITING A FEW NUMBERS DOWN, YOU CAN RUIN OUR WHOLE WEEK. WE BOW TO YOUR AUTHORITY, O MIGHTY ONE. OUR ENDLESS RESPECT NOTWITHSTANDING, YOU ARE PARKED IN THE MIDDLE OF THE FUCKING STREET. YOU DRIVE—AND PARK—LIKE AN ASSHOLE.

BEST,

_____

DEAR PARKING—
ENFORCEMENT ASSHOLE

Dear Unmarked-Police-
Car Asshole,

You're not fooling anyone. I know you're a
cop. Are you on a stakeout? Why are you
creeping around? Are you going to pull me
over? What should I do? Your presence is
very disconcerting. Is a robbery taking place
right behind me? Am I about to be taken
hostage? Why are you slowly going through
that stop sign, turning right, and looking
around? What's going to happen?! WHY
WON'T YOU TELL ME?! WEIRD COPS IN
UNMARKED COP CARS REALLY FREAK
ME OUT. You drive like an asshole.

Legally yours,

_____

P.S. I bet you know all the best 24-hour
diners in the area, don't you?

Dear Unmarked-
Police-Car Asshole

Dear Asshole in the
Multipurpose Power
Company Vehicle,

Just what are you doing in that
strange, multipurpose vehicle? You sure
have a lot of weird things hanging
off the side. Can I pull around you?
I hate being behind you. I don't know
if your vehicle is going to explode or
what it's going to do. Maybe it's fake,
and you're actually some criminal
about to pull off a big heist. Maybe
you're the jerk those undercover cops
are looking for. I can't stand the
tension! Will you put out your orange
cones already and do something? Why
am I so concerned about you? You're
just some overpaid civic employee who
drives like an asshole.

Civic-mindedly yours,

_____

P.S. Do you have a dental plan?
Because your teeth are a mess.

Dear Asshole
in the Multipurpose
Power Company Vehicle

Dear Presidential-Motorcade Asshole,

Look, I get it. You feel bad about what happened to JFK. We all do. You probably look back on that day and think, "If only they had a few more cars, maybe things would have turned out differently." But this long-as-fuck motorcade begs the question—just how many cars do you need to transport one guy? I'm under the impression that our commander-in-chief (A) is a normal-size human being, and (B) rides in a car that is built like a tank. Why does the entire city need to be shut down every time he goes to a fund-raiser?

We're all late for work now, every single one of us. No president is worth the congestion you've caused today. Not Lincoln. Certainly not Taft. I hope you crash and die a fiery death, but the president emerges unscathed from the wreckage because to wish anything otherwise is illegal. You—and the fifty cars behind you—drive like assholes.

Salutations,

_____

P.S. Please don't put me on some weird list that makes the IRS audit me.

Dear Presidential-
Motorcade Asshole

Dear Asshole in the Fire Truck Taking Up Fourteen Spaces,

Hey, I get it—firemen risk their lives to keep us safe. But do you have to take up fourteen fucking parking spaces at a fucking taco stand? What the fuck?! I'll get the tacos for you and drop them off at the fucking fire station. Sure, I admit, I'm a little jealous because my girlfriend is saying, "Oooh, look at the firemen," as I'm driving aimlessly around, looking for a parking space. So do me a favor and quit lollygagging and tanning your muscles. Get your fucking tacos, and free up those fourteen spaces so the rest of us can park and eat some fucking tacos! You park like an asshole.

Move it or lose it,

_____

Dear Asshole in the Fire Truck
Taking Up Fourteen Spaces

Dear Asshole Taking Up Two Spaces,

I'm not familiar with any country where you are allowed to park your car right over one of the solid lines in a parking lot. The solid line is a demarcation of TWO spaces. The solid line isn't meant to bisect your fucking car. I suppose at the turn of the last century, we could have made that rule. Yeah, maybe that may have worked, sure. But, it's now been a rule for *one hundred fucking years*—everywhere on the planet! So, YES, parking on the fucking line makes you an asshole!

Your brain is broken,

_____

Dear Asshole Taking
Up Two Spaces

Dear Asshole Who Made It Impossible for Me to Open My Car Door,

I'll wait. No really, I'll wait for you. I'm curious if your face is as detestable as I imagine it to be. I want to see the shiny, bloated, Frisbee face that couldn't be bothered to take two seconds to examine your surroundings and repark your car. I'd like to know what was so pressing that you had to rush to park, with nary a thought of the car next to you. Let me guess: Late to a court-ordered meeting? Lenny Kravitz autograph signing? Tater tot sale at Sonic for Frisbee-faced fuckwads? Whatever it was, I've lost my patience and now have to enter my car through the passenger door. Thanks a lot, asshole.

Frustratingly,

_____

Dear Asshole Who Made It
Impossible for Me to
Open My Car Door

Dear Double-Parked Asshole,

Is it an emergency? Can I help? Are you stalled? Oh, you're entitled! Are you a member of the royal family, with a special, royal errand to do? Why look for a parking space when you can just inconvenience everyone else around you? I curse you. May your car be perpetually keyed by annoyed citizens. May all the people you have inconvenienced rise up and attack your car, ripping it apart and leaving you there with only a driver's seat and a steering wheel. You drive like an asshole.

Hopefully,

_____

Dear Double-Parked Asshole

Dear Asshole Who Blocked Me In,

I would understand if I were some fugitive, some mafia kingpin about to be assassinated, or someone about to be murdered. But I am none of these things. I am just some Joe who went out to get eggs, and now here I am waiting for about a month to get out of my parking space because you blocked me in. Now come back out and let me leave this fucking space! I'm sure you must look like an asshole, and you most assuredly *park* like one.

Stewing in my own juices,

_____

Dear Asshole Who Blocked Me In

Dear Aggressive Parallel-Parking Asshole,

Hey, what do you think you're doing?! Are you having a psychotic meltdown, or maybe you just can't parallel park for shit? You're hitting the cars around you. Oh, I get it—you're slowly pulling in, and your plan is to inch back and forth thirty times to fit into that tiny parking space. You're about to give me a heart attack. You've already bumped my car sixteen times in ten seconds. I can't wait for the day that you hit someone tougher, bigger, and less afraid than me. You parallel-park like an asshole.

Squeamishly yours,

_____

Dear Aggressive
Parallel-Parking Asshole

Dear Non-Parallel-Parking, Cowardly Asshole,

Oh my God. Oh my God. Oh my God. Oh my God. Oh my God. Will you park your fucking car already?! What makes someone who's so scared of something insist on doing it? You're like the kid at the pool who stands on the diving board, too scared to jump but not moving out of the way, ruining everyone's day. I don't have forty-five minutes to wait behind you as you gingerly try to parallel-park. Go take driver's ed again or something. You park like an asshole.

Late because you suck,

_____

Dear Non-Parallel-Parking,
Cowardly Asshole

Dear Texting-and-Never-Leaving Asshole,

I'll give you a second. I'm sure you're texting something important. You're probably giving an ETA to your kids or your sick grandmother. Might want to wrap it up soon. Lot's pretty full, and I got a line of cars behind me. Seriously, how long does it take to text, "Leaving now"? I just did it in eight seconds. There, I did it again. You've been texting for a solid two minutes now. What other information must be urgently conveyed from the parking structure of this Target?

Are you writing *The Godfather?* Not the script for the movie, but the original Mario Puzo novel? Because even Mario Puzo took breaks from writing to eat, sleep, and, yes, drive. Or are you writing a work of even greater length and import? OK fuck this! I'm moving on to another space, but please remember to list me in the acknowledgments of your very long novel. You text, park, and drive like an asshole!

Patiently,

_____

Dear Texting-and-Never-
Leaving Asshole

Dear Anal-Grocery-Packer Asshole,

Hi. See me waiting over here? I'm the one with a bunch of cars clogged behind me. Why? Because I'm waiting for you to pull out of that spot so I can pull into it. All you have to do is pack your groceries into your trunk. Yup, that's all you have to do. But I see you are one of those annoying anal types who plays Tetris with his grocery bags to get them in just the right way. Do you realize there are other people waiting? Last time I checked, there wasn't an award for perfect grocery packing. In fact, could you step aside? I'd like to smash into your car over and over again, destroying all of your meticulously placed groceries in the process. You park and probably drive like an asshole.

Seething,

_____

Dear Anal-Grocery-
Packer Asshole

Dear Asshole with the Huge Mountain of Scrap Metal in the Back of Your Shitty Pickup Truck,

I wish you could experience the terror of driving behind you. Are you in some sort of contest where you see how high you can pile dangerous metal in the smallest, crummiest truck that's ready to break down? You drive as if you have a thousand gallons of nitroglycerine in your stupid little pickup truck. As far as I know, you do. I do know that no one else could drive that strange jalopy with a Jenga-styled metal stack in the back. But still, I must point this out to you: You drive like an asshole!

Constructively,

_____

Dear Asshole with the Huge Mountain of Scrap Metal in the Back of Your Shitty Pickup Truck

Dear Lawn-Care-Crew Asshole,

Look, I know things didn't turn out well for you. I'm sure you're not a medical student just doing this for the summer, but don't take this out on me. I know you're mad at the world. But how's about not slowly driving through the neighborhood with a bunch of grass-stained convicts creepily glaring at passersby? Because when you do, it must be said, you are driving like an asshole.

Cautiously,

_____

Dear Lawn-Care-
Crew Asshole

Dear Furniture-Moving Asshole,

Oh, I get it. I saw you driving around the neighborhood looking for an address. Seems innocent enough. Except you're in a huge fucking truck! Here's an idea: Park the truck and look for the address on foot so that you don't have to ruin everyone's day by making nineteen-point turns while trying to deliver a sofa. Thanks for taking up the whole street and making our lives that much more difficult. You drive like an asshole.

Annoyed,

_____

Dear Furniture-
Moving Asshole

Dear Asshole on the Freeway with Shit Flying Off His Truck,

How fun it must be to load a bunch of loose junk into the back of an open truck and then drive on the freeway at 100 miles an hour to watch it fly off. Oh look, the guy in the convertible next to me was scalped by a flying something or other. Maybe you are just a modern-day Hansel and Gretel, leaving a trail of bullshit all over the freeway so we can come find and rescue you. Except no one will, because you drive like an asshole.

Have a wonderful day,

_____

Dear Asshole on the Freeway
with Shit Flying Off His Truck

Dear Tow-Truck Asshole,

You're speeding while towing a car?! How would you feel if you turned a corner and flung off that car, and it smashed into a store? From the look on your face, you'd probably just mutter, "Oooh, neat." I do not agree with the policy of thawing out cavemen, having them train for one day, and then making them tow-truck drivers. You've already ruined some poor schmuck's day, no doubt, by towing away his innocently parked car. And now you're trying to ruin even more lives by flying down the highway. You, sir, drive like a complete asshole.

Humanly yours,

_____

Dear Tow-Truck Asshole

Dear Beer-Truck Asshole,

I get it. You're the third-most-important truck there is. Fire truck, then ambulance, then beer truck. But do you have to park in the middle of the fucking road and unload your beer in that weird, cocky, cavalier way? I resent the fact that I'm more scared to hit you than you are to be hit. What's the life expectancy of a beer-truck driver? Is it the same as a machine gunner in Vietnam? Because, believe me, most of the assholes on this road are going to swerve to avoid hitting that beer . . . and you. You drive, park, and deliver beer like an asshole.

Thoughtfully,

_____

Dear Beer-Truck Asshole

Dear Beer-Truck Asshole,

I get it. You're the third-most-important truck there is. Fire truck, then ambulance, then beer truck. But do you have to park in the middle of the fucking road and unload your beer in that weird, cocky, cavalier way? I resent the fact that I'm more scared to hit you than you are to be hit. What's the life expectancy of a beer-truck driver? Is it the same as a machine gunner in Vietnam? Because, believe me, most of the assholes on this road are going to swerve to avoid hitting that beer . . . and you. You drive, park, and deliver beer like an asshole.

Thoughtfully,

_____

Dear Beer-Truck Asshole

Dear Power-Company Asshole,

Thanks for changing the transformer, but I'd like to address the man with the open mouth who also works for the power company and is just staring up at the guy working: You're standing in the road. Does this mean I should go around you? You're holding up traffic. Maybe some sort of eye contact? Maybe some sort of signal? Don't you have one of those neat paddles that says "slow" on one side and "stop" on the other? Is it that fucking hard? Are you sad that you'll never get to change transformers yourself someday, because you're too fucking stupid? Oh good, you're getting in the truck now. Surely, you're about to clear the way for us drivers.

Nope. You've just adjusted your giant truck into a position that ensures traffic from both sides of the road is now fucked. At least now you get to sit down in your driver's seat. All the openmouthed breathing and looking up can really wear a guy out. Have another doughnut, since it seems you lost half of the one you ate earlier in your stupid mustache.

Painfully yours,

_____

Dear Power-Company Asshole

Dear Birthday-Party-Clown Asshole,

Let's put aside the fact that what you do is considered strange and dubious behavior by everyone else's standards. Do you really need to plaster the side of your red Dodge Caravan with ridiculous advertisements for your party-clown services? Is that a picture of your face, or did a Brillo pad get stuck to a wet pillow? But I guess it's best to get your name out there. Right, Frizzo? I would think party-clowning would be more of a referral-based, Craigslist-ad type of business. Isn't that part of the curriculum at clown college? Did you even graduate from clown college?! I think it's time to unwrap the car and keep your fetishistic obsession between you and your misguided clients. Most of us have no trouble keeping our creepiness to ourselves. Try it sometime, asshole.

Forever scared,

_____

Dear Birthday-Party-
Clown Asshole

Dear Food-Truck Asshole,

Oh good, you brought your kitchen out onto the highway. If you're going to drive 45, could you at least toss me one of those artisan breakfast empanadas? You might want to drive faster—the Ethiopian meatball truck is racing to the same burned-out sandlot next to that killer local music festival and is sure to cut into your business. There are only so many dumb assholes looking to line up in the cold to buy their food from some weird half-restaurant, half-UPS-truck thing. You've got to get to those assholes fast! Hurry up, asshole!

Insincerely,

_____

Dear Food-Truck asshole

Dear Food-Delivery Asshole,

Look, I know it's embarrassing to drive one of the cheapest cars available and to have that accentuated by some strange, lit-up logo on top of it. I know you're working for tips and you want to get the food there hot and fast, but you'd think someone who drives for a living would somehow get better with all that practice! How can you drive ten hours a day and still be that shitty of a driver? Perhaps the smell of whatever awful food you're carrying is distracting enough to cause you to continuously keep swerving into my lane. Are you doing it on purpose? Is it a joke? That, I might understand. Here's a tip: You drive like an asshole.

Kind regards,

_____

Dear Food-Delivery Asshole

Dear United-States-Postal-Worker Asshole,

OK, you're a postal worker. I know all the jokes. I know all the clichés. But you have the greatest gig. You're not slogging along inside the post office or walking a long route. You're one of the lucky ones who got a cool mail truck, with the steering wheel on the wrong side and everything! All you have to do is remain seated, roll down your window, and put mail in people's mailboxes way out here in idyllic Anytown, USA. Not sure how you can fuck that up, but you've found a way! You inch along for no reason and with that stupid look on your face. No one can pass you because you hog the road with your weird, wide vehicle that probably cost taxpayers a million dollars!

Is it some sacred point of pride for every postal worker to be amazingly lazy? Is your actual foot so apathetic that it can't even press down on the gas pedal? I don't want to kick someone when they're down, but I guess all that post-office shit is true. You stumbling, idiotic, lazy, clueless fuck. Society can't go paperless fast enough so moronic dinosaurs like you can be put out to pasture. You drive like an asshole.

Coldly,

_____

P.S. If and when you decide to go "postal," please take aim at yourself first.

Dear United-States-Postal-
Worker Asshole

SHITTY-CAR OWNERS

They're the Owners of the Shittiest Cars on the Road—Does That Also Mean They Have to Be the Shittiest Drivers?

Dear Asshole with the Duct-Taped-On Fender,

Hey, psychopath: I'm glad you saved enough duct tape to tape on that fender. Too bad you only have half a roll left for your kidnap victims now. Do you ever plan on getting that fender fixed? Doesn't look like it. Just looking at your dent-filled, taped-together wreck of a car, nothing could be more obvious than the fact that you drive like an asshole. I've got my eye on you.

Watching,

Dear Asshole with the
Duct-Taped-On Fender

Dear Asshole with the Smashed Taillight That "Cleverly" Has Red Cellophane Taped over It,

Great work—I guess that's legal. It's so distracting seeing one red taillight and that other, reddish-pinkish one. What is that, red cellophane from a candy apple or something? I don't mind that you had to take some emergency action to make your taillight work, and I don't mind that you obviously are never going to get it fixed. I just hate the stupid, hateful look on your face, driving around beaming like this is the best work you've ever done—taping that stupid red cellophane over your taillight.

Congratulations, you've really accomplished something in your life. It's never going to get any better for you. Enjoy it while it lasts. By the looks of the rest of your car, that should be about thirty days—or maybe less—because you drive like an asshole.

Admiringly,

_____

Dear Asshole with the Smashed Taillight That "Cleverly" Has Red Cellophane Taped over It

DEAR ASSHOLE DRIVING ON A MINI SPARE TIRE,

I NOTICED YOU'VE GOT ONE OF THOSE LITTLE MINI DOUGHNUT TIRES. THOSE SURE COME IN HANDY. YOU DO KNOW THOSE ARE JUST MEANT TO BE USED TO DRIVE IMMEDIATELY TO THE TIRE PLACE TO BUY A REAL TIRE FOR YOUR CAR, RIGHT? YOU SEEM TO BE DRIVING IT ALL WILLY-NILLY. ARE YOU IN A CONTEST TO SEE HOW FAR YOU CAN DRIVE ON IT? DO ME A FAVOR: STOP RUNNING YOUR ERRANDS AND JUST DRIVE STRAIGHT TO THE TIRE PLACE. I HOPE ALL THREE OF YOUR OTHER TIRES COMMIT SUICIDE AND EXPLODE, LEAVING YOU ON THE SIDE OF THE ROAD LIKE THE JERK THAT YOU ARE. YOU DRIVE LIKE AN ASSHOLE.

SPARINGLY,

_____

DEAR ASSHOLE DRIVING
ON A MINI SPARE TIRE

Dear Asshole with a Garbage Bag Taped over Your Window,

Wow, you make the guy with the red cellophane taped over his taillight look like a genius. You've taped a garbage bag over a broken window, and I can see that you have no plans to fix it anytime soon. If your windshield were smashed, would you just tape a garbage bag over that, too, and continue to drive? I think you just might. Your brain is probably not smaller than a walnut, but no way is it bigger than a baseball. Do you have any idea what kind of a fucking asshole you look like, driving around with a fucking bag duct-taped to your window like that? Probably not. You look and drive like a fucking asshole.

Amazed,

_____

Dear Asshole with a
Garbage Bag Taped
over Your Window

Dear Asshole Driving the Eco-Friendly, Oil-Powered, Modified Car,

You dirty, smug hippy. I feel like I'm driving behind a shitty fast-food restaurant that hasn't changed its french-fry oil in weeks. I hate the way that engine sounds. I hate the way it smells. I hate the way you wear your hair. I'm sure you're wearing some kind of stupid little pointy shoes to press that gas pedal down. I hope your brakes give out and you wipe out all of your friends in their stupid little drum circle at the bottom of the hill. You really drive like an asshole.

Be well,

_____

*Dear Asshole Driving
the Eco-Friendly,
Oil-Powered, Modified Car*

Dear Asshole Who Continues to Drive on a Flat Tire,

Excuse me! But do you at all hear the FLAP FLAP FLAP FLAP FLAP FLAP FLAP FLAP FLAP FLAP FLAP FLAP FLAP FLAP FLAP FLAP FLAP FLAP FLAP sound of the tire you're driving on? You do realize you are doing far more damage to your car than the cost of a new tire, right? Are you having some kind of nervous breakdown? If yes, I'm sorry. If not, you're driving like an asshole.

Concerned,

_____

Dear Asshole Who
Continues to Drive
on a Flat Tire

Dear Asshole with the
Black Smoke Coming Out
of Your Vehicle,

I think I've solved global warming. It's not really all the SUVs, Humvees, fighter jets, and oil refineries. It's really just you and your amazingly poor-running engine. I should know—I just drove in the lane behind you for three minutes, and I'm sure I just cut five years off my life. I feel like I've just smoked ten thousand packs of cigarettes. Are you the devil, slowly killing the earth? It's funny—you never know what form Satan will come in. I never thought he'd be some dweeby moron driving his crummy car around. You drive like *an* asshole.

Unkind regards,

———————————————

Dear Asshole with the
Black Smoke Coming
Out of Your Vehicle

Dear Fenderless Asshole,

Are you on a crime spree? Was your fender ripped off when you robbed that bank and hit that cop car, and now you're in another county, lying low? Well, it's kind of hard to lie low when you have no fenders. Why is it that every time I see some fucked-up, fenderless asshole like you, I just know you're never going to get that car fixed—are you? And you're eventually going to do something really stupid in that car and break something. Don't take this the wrong way, but I hope your engine catches on fire. You'll have to drive into the ocean to put it out, you'll get swept away, and no one will ever see you again because you drive like an asshole.

Wishing you well,

_____

Dear Fenderless Asshole

TEXTERS AND PHONE USERS

Not Just Limited to Asshole Teenagers

Dear Red-Light-Texting Asshole,

I know you're waiting at a red light, because I'm waiting behind you and I can see you're texting. I can see the stupid grin on your face and your fingers moving. Oh look, the light is green, everyone else is going, and you're still typing away, looking for the right emoji, and now I have to be the asshole who beeps at you. Doesn't this happen to you all day, every day? I can't wait until that new law is passed for people who text at red lights. You know, the one where their foreheads get tattooed with: "I text and drive like an asshole."

LOL,

_____

t

d

ad
al
uilt
om
ke
ots
t of
gla

Dear Red-Light-
Texting Asshole

Dear Texting-Teen Asshole,

First of all, you're a teenager. You don't know how to fucking drive yet, but I'm sure you're a world-class texter. I'm sure your attention span is fucked already, and you've got really, really important shit to text while driving. Gosh, I wish I knew your number because I'd send you some of the many, many PSAs about texting and driving. Maybe you could watch them on some train tracks. You stupid texting teen, you drive like an asshole.

<3 U,

_____

Dear Texting-Teen Asshole

DEAR TEXTING-COP ASSHOLE,

SO, LET ME GET THIS STRAIGHT: YOU CAN PULL ME OVER WHEN I'M LOOKING AT THE MAP ON MY PHONE AND TICKET ME FOR TEXTING, BUT YOU, KIND OFFICER, ARE ALLOWED TO TEXT SMACK-DAB IN THE MIDDLE OF THE INTERSECTION WITHOUT FEAR OF PUNISHMENT?

LET'S CUT THE BULLSHIT RIGHT NOW. IT'S HIGHLY UNLIKELY YOU'RE CONDUCTING POLICE BUSINESS OVER YOUR PERSONAL iPHONE. UNLESS THE RULES HAVE CHANGED SIGNIFICANTLY SINCE THE PRE-SMARTPHONE DAYS OF COPS, YOU USE RADIOS FOR POLICE BUSINESS. SO I DON'T WANT TO HEAR ANY EXCUSES, BUSTER BROWN.

ASSUREDLY, THIS IS A RELATIVELY SMALL COMPLAINT IN THE GRAND SCHEME OF COMPLAINTS FILED AGAINST LAW ENFORCEMENT. BUT BIG INJUSTICES SPRING FROM LITTLE INJUSTICES, SO WHY DON'T WE NIP THIS TEXTING DOUBLE STANDARD IN THE BUD RIGHT NOW? PUT THE PHONE DOWN, OFFICER! PUT YOUR HANDS ON THE WHEEL WHERE I CAN SEE THEM! NOW, MOTHERFUCKER, NOW! THIS IS A CITIZEN'S ARREST FOR DRIVING LIKE AN ASSHOLE!

RESPECTFULLY,

_____

DEAR TEXTING-COP ASSHOLE

Dear Texting-Mom Asshole,

May I commend you, Madam. Your young children see you texting and driving, and now they inherently have a living example of what not to do. Some people are sour on the new generation, but now it's the young children in your car who know how stupid their mom is. Texting with a carload of kids—that's great. If they defy the odds and live to see adulthood, they can always look at you as the best case study of how NOT to live life. You, Madam, drive and text like an asshole.

,

_____

Dear Texting-Mom Asshole

Dear Hands-Free, Gesticulating Asshole,

Is there a bee loose in your car? Are you swatting at something? No, you're just some greasy Hollywood agent talking on his hands-free device. Or are you rehearsing lines for a movie in which you play Hitler? What the fuck is wrong with you? You're the only person I've ever seen whom I'd rather see texting while driving than talking to himself. I don't know what you're freaking out about, but calm the fuck down because you drive like an asshole.

Thanks for your consideration,

_____

Dear Hands-Free,
Gesticulating Asshole

Dear Asshole Getting Directions from Someone on the Phone While Driving,

I can tell from the way you're holding the phone to your head, driving slowly, and looking around, seemingly ready to turn at any moment, that you're getting directions from someone on the phone while you're also trying to drive. I can only imagine this conversation. How are they going to help you when they don't know where you fucking are?! Can't you just get a fucking address?! You look like some scared idiot who's at the controls of a plane after the pilot has just died of a heart attack and the control tower is talking you down. Please start the descent already. Your passengers have places to be.. Boy, you sure do drive like an asshole.

Deepest sympathies,

_____

Dear Asshole Getting
Directions from Someone on
the Phone While Driving

RVs, BOAT TRAILERS, AND SNOWMOBILE HAULERS

Dear Speedboat-Hauling Asshole,

Nice speedboat, asshole. I'm sure you can't wait to get out into the open water so you can pop a brewski and take a few selfies in your ratty, old Mets hat. That makes you cool. People might even think you fish, which would be even cooler. You don't fish, though, do you? You just careen around the harbor, wondering why this didn't turn into the party boat you imagined. Unfortunately, most spring-breakers don't want to hang out with Captain Dad on his edgy new speedboat, do they? Even though you're the one paying for the beer. Ouch.

It must really be difficult gauging how long your kick-ass party boat drags from your F-150. I get it: You're not trained to haul massive cargo. Perhaps, then, it's time to retire this monstrosity before you drag its propeller over my hood. Isn't your midlife crisis over yet? Maybe there's still time to make your family love you again. Or maybe not, asshole.

Unconcerned,

_____

Dear Speedboat-Hauling Asshole

Dear Asshole Hauling a Horse Trailer,

Sure, I'll just stare at your horse's sphincter for the next hour while I'm stuck behind you on this country road. Really? There's poop falling out of it now? Fantastic. I was really hoping to smell that today. There's no way you're going to let me pass, are you? You probably can't even see me drifting along behind your shitting Clydesdale. That's OK. I'll just stay back here, wondering when the huge captive beast defecating in the cage in front of me is going to finally lose its mind and jump through my windshield. Hey, at least this stinky drive would be over. Thanks for the eyeful of asshole, asshole.

PEW,

_____

Dear Asshole Hauling
a Horse Trailer

Dear Super-Tailgater Asshole Hauling a Custom Barbecue,

What kind of fucking monstrosity is this? I'm sure you take great pride in this custom barbecue thing you have built, so I take it that's why you are driving so slowly. You're not driving the Popemobile in some procession. You're not driving a hearse carrying some world leader to a huge funeral. You're not even driving a float loaded with clowns or whoever the fuck rides on a stupid float. In all of these scenarios, the streets would be blocked off for you, and you would be allowed to go five miles an hour. But you are just pulling a fucking experimental-meat-smoker party wagon for your own pleasure. I'm sure you had to wake up eighteen hours before the game so that you could inch your way there while your precious meat smokes. I hope your overblown weenie roast gives everyone diarrhea and they shit their pants right as the other team kicks a winning field goal, because you drive like an asshole.

Go team,

_____

Dear Super-Tailgater
Asshole Hauling a
Custom Barbecue

Dear Asshole Camping Family,

Why has the freeway become one extremely fast
left lane and one excruciatingly slow right lane?
Because the happy family with their monster
RV is clogging it all up!! I bet by the time your
ridiculous cross-country, circus-caravan nightmare
is almost ending you will have just started getting
the hang of driving this bizarre family freak show.
Do us all a favor, including yourself: Pull over,
set the thing on fire, and send your kids to camp.
I know you are all sick of looking at each other.
Stop pretending this is working. You are driving
like an asshole.

Safe travels,

_____

Dear Asshole Camping Family

Dear Asshole Driving an RV and Towing a Secondary Vehicle That is Better Than My Everyday Car,

Look at me! I have a great RV that's better than most people's homes. It has all of the luxuries you could ever want, and I can drive it into town. With all these amazing creature comforts around me, I guess I forget that I am in a huge, box-shaped bus, hauling another car behind me as I happily zigzag in and out of lanes, cutting people off. HA! Isn't life wonderful?

I hope your extra car gets stolen and your RV's sewage tank ruptures, disturbing the beehive that is hopefully forming in the convenient luggage compartment. I hope these bees sting all of you until you bloat up like balloon people and are stuck inside your RV until the swelling goes down. I hate you and your perfect vacation. You are making me late for WORK because you are driving like an asshole.

Have a nice trip,

_____

P.S. I hope you like the picture of the penis I just spray-painted on the side of your RV.

Dear Asshole Driving an RV and Towing a Secondary Vehicle That is Better Than My Everyday Car

VANITY-PLATE ASSHOLES

*Personal Vanity Plates and the
Assholes Who Obtain Them*

DEAR "THIS IS WHAT I DO FOR
A LIVING" VANITY-PLATE ASSHOLE,

HEY, IS "DOKTRR" WHAT YOU DO FOR A LIVING?
AMAZING! I'M SO HONORED TO BE DRIVING
NEAR YOU. GOSH, CAN I ASK HOW YOU GOT TO
BE SO SUCCESSFUL? IF YOU DIDN'T HAVE THAT
PLATE THAT ADVERTISED YOUR SACRED, STUPID
PROFESSION TO THE WORLD, I WOULD HAVE
THOUGHT YOU WERE JUST A REGULAR CITIZEN
LIKE ME. WHAT A CRIME! THANK YOU FOR YOUR
CLEVER, CLEVER PLATE. NOW WE KNOW HOW
SPECIAL YOU REALLY ARE! BY ALL MEANS, CUT
IN FRONT OF ME. AFTER ALL, YOU CERTAINLY
ARE BETTER THAN THE REST OF US. YOU DRIVE
LIKE AN ASSHOLE!

FU,

DEAR "THIS IS WHA[T]
I DO FOR A LIVING["]
VANITY-PLATE ASS[H]OLE

DEAR VNTY-PLT ASSHL,

WHO CRES ABT UR LIFE? WHO CRES WHT U LKE? NBDY DOES! R U INSCRE? IZZAT Y U DO THS? YER PTHTIC. MYBE U NEED THRPY. BED WTTR? MAMAS BOY? DPRESSD?

YER NOT CLVR. NBDY LKS U. Y ADVRTSE UR BNG A FCKHEAD? U STNK. UR STPID. SHT FR BRNS. JMP OFF A BRDGE. U DRVE LKE AN ASSHL!

SNCRLY,

_____

DEAR VNTY-PLT ASSHL

Dear "What the Hell Does That Even Mean?" Vanity-Plate Asshole,

I don't get it. Are we supposed to get it? Do *you* get it? Should anyone get it? Isn't it supposed to be a recognizable phrase? Or a slogan? It bugs me. What does it mean? Are you in a secret society? Don't you know that everyone around you is looking at it, wondering what it means? Do you take pleasure in that? You know that makes everyone around you drive like an asshole, and therefore, YOU drive like an asshole.

Confused and angry,

_____

P.S. I've decided I don't care what it means. But you still drive like a huge asshole.

Dear "What the Hell
Does That Even Mean?"
Vanity-Plate Asshole

Dear Asshole Who Thinks He Has a Cool Vanity Plate,

Hey, real cool vanity plate, but I think you could have done better. Was SMUGFUK already taken? That's OK—you still come off like a major DOOSHBG. DHRREA FACE could be good for a second car. How about E4ESUCK? That would have been a good one for you. Actually, the one you picked is really amazing. You really couldn't be a bigger asshole!

Congratulations,

_____

Dear Asshole Who Thinks
He Has a Cool Vanity Plate

Dear Asshole with the Shitty Car and Shitty Vanity Plate,

Why would you get a vanity plate when you have such a shit car? Are you being ironic? Do you have a great sense of humor about yourself? Ha ha, my lack of ambition and earning power must be captured in a catchphrase! I will champion my right to be mediocre. My sense of humor makes me special.

Can't you feel the sour looks around you? Why don't you get a tattoo across your face that says, "Regular person with a great sense of humor"? That would be a bit more clever, no? Take your fucking vanity-plate money and get your fucking fender fixed. You drive like an asshole.

Distastefully yours,

Dear Asshole with the Shitty Car and Shitty Vanity Plate

CAR DECORATORS

*Special Idiots Who Have
to Flaunt Their Religious
and Political Affiliations
on Their Bumpers*

DEAR BUMPER-STICKER-LADEN, RIGHT-WING-
CLICHÉ, SUV-DRIVING ASSHOLE,

THANK GOD YOU HAVE THAT HUGE SUV TO DRIVE ALL ALONE
IN. IT'S JUST YOU AND YOUR OPINIONS, BLARING OFF THE BACK
OF YOUR TRUCK THROUGH ALL YOUR STUPID BUMPER STICKERS.
I GUESS THERE'S NO MORE ROOM FOR ANYONE ELSE. WE GET
IT ALREADY. YOU LIKE GUNS AND JESUS AND CORPORATIONS.
EVERYONE IS ENTITLED TO THEIR OPINION, BUT WHY IS IT THAT
THE MOST OPINIONATED KNOW-IT-ALLS LIKE YOU SEEM TO HAVE
THAT WEIRD, OPENMOUTHED STARE THAT MAKES IT SEEM LIKE
THEY HAVE BRAIN DAMAGE?

ARE YOU SURE YOUR EXHAUST ISN'T LEAKING INTO YOUR CAR?
OR ARE YOU JUST A WEIRD, SHAVEN GORILLA THAT SOMEHOW
HAS A LICENSE? MAYBE YOU DON'T HAVE A LICENSE. ACTUALLY,
I THINK A GORILLA WOULD BE MORE SENSITIVE TO OTHER
PEOPLE ON THE ROAD. IN FACT, I THINK REPLACING YOU WITH
A GORILLA WOULD BE A BENEFIT IN EVERY CONCEIVABLE WAY.
AT LEAST MOST GORILLAS DON'T THINK THERE'S A WAR ON
CHRISTMAS. YOU DRIVE LIKE AN ASSHOLE.

LIBERALLY YOURS,

_____

DEAR BUMPER-STICKER-LADEN, RIGHT-WING-CLICHÉ, SUV-DRIVING ASSHOLE

Dear Bumper-Sticker-Laden, Left-Wing-Cliché, Hybrid-Driving Asshole,

I really appreciate you saving the world with your slightly higher gas mileage. If only everyone knew exactly what was wrong with the world and how to fix it, like you do! Perhaps if you turned down the local public radio station on your way to the vegan co-op swap meet, you might drive a little more courteously. I know you must have a lot on your mind now that your son with the gender-neutral name is up for admittance into the most highly touted and prestigious preschool in town. But, please! Keep those worries back home at your converted warehouse loft space, not on the road.

It's funny: I know your intentions are to change the world with your powerful bumper-sticker messages, yet somehow I feel like I want to become more right wing after seeing you. Something about your stupid little head and the way you drive your know-it-all machine. I never in my life dreamed I would want to purchase a pickup truck with a gun rack until I saw you. Could you please do me a favor and drive your slow, pretentious, hyper-mileage hybrid straight up your own asshole? Because that's exactly how you drive: like an asshole.

Please choke on your limited emissions,

_____

Dear Bumper-Sticker-Laden,
Left-Wing-Cliché,
Hybrid-Driving Asshole

Dear Proud-to-Be-from-Texas-Bumper-Sticker Asshole,

Wow, you're from Texas?! That's amazing!! You mean the place with the guns and the cowboys? The place with all the beef? Border patrol?! Oil?! The Gulf of Mexico?! Ross Perot and Lee Harvey Oswald?! THE PLACE WITH ALL THE FISHIN' 'N' SHOOTIN' 'N' MOONSHININ'?! Hee haw, lookie here, Jessup, that open country dun' dere's as purty as a wash bucket bass line snappin' away in the cool, desert night. Let's go a-fishin' for some crawdads 'cause, y'know, they always come a-nippin' when the sun's just a-settin'! YEEE HAW!!

Good day,

_____

P.S. You forgot to remind me not to mess with Texas, asshole.

Dear Proud-to-Be-
from-Texas-Bumper-
Sticker Asshole

Dear Proud Asshole Parent of an Honor Student,

You're an embarrassment to your child. Let me be clear: There is not a universe in which your child looks at your bumper sticker as a point of pride. To her, it is a pox on her coolness. You might as well have a bumper sticker reading: "My Child Pisses the Bed" or "My Child Lacks Sufficient Hand-Eye Coordination" or "I Wish to Place Hurdles Between My Child and the Opposite Sex." Because that's what you're saying with your bumper sticker.

Also, not to bury the lede, but verily I say unto you: Nobody cares. I don't know your child. I don't care about his/her/its grades. I have friends and loved ones with fluctuating health and dim job prospects whom I rarely check in with. Why would I care about your kid's GPA? I barely cared about my own GPA in school.

If you want to do something for your child, lead by example and stop coming to abrupt stops in traffic, stop looking at your stupid phone, and stop yelling at your brats in the car! You drive—and parent—like an asshole.

Scoldingly yours,

_____

Dear Proud Asshole Parent
of an Honor Student

DEAR ASSHOLE LOVER OF SO MANY
COOL, COOL BANDS,

I SEE THAT YOU ARE REALLY INTO MUSIC! SO MANY
GREAT WINDOW DECALS AND BUMPER STICKERS—I LOVE
PEOPLE WHO HAVE A PASSION FOR STUFF. I REALLY DO.
HEY! I KNOW WHAT YOU SHOULD HAVE A PASSION FOR!
HOW'S ABOUT HAVING A PASSION FOR NOT DRIVING LIKE
AN AIRHEADED, WANDERING DUMB FUCK?! LIFE ISN'T A
FUCKING FESTIVAL, MAN! YOUR CAR SUCKS! YOU CAN'T
DRIVE! YOUR NEW, RETRO-TRENDY '70S COMB-OVER,
MESSED-UP HIPSTER HAIRSTYLE WITH THE IN-VOGUE
BEARD IS SOOO STUPID! THE OLD BANDS YOU LIKE
WERE NEVER GOOD. THE NEW ONES YOU LIKE ARE
SHITTY. YOU HAVE TERRIBLE TASTE IN MUSIC, AND YOU
DRIVE LIKE AN ASSHOLE.

PEACE,

_____

DEAR ASSHOLE LOVER
OF SO MANY COOL, COOL BANDS

Dear Asshole Who Hates Saddam Hussein,

Well, I have some good news and some bad news.

The good news is: We got him. Saddam, that is. Caught and hung about a decade ago—it's possible you missed it. I get it—you're busy not washing your car. You don't have time to follow the news, but rest easy. Saddam is no longer on the lam, torturing his own people with abandon. He's a dead man.

The bad news is the war was a doozy and things didn't exactly calm down immediately after we nabbed Saddam. So when you (drunkenly) drive that car to the liquor store for a refill, you might want to consider the fact that your "Saddam Insane" bumper sticker might be conjuring up some rather unpleasant memories for other motorists. It would be like renting a billboard in 1964 to tell everyone we need to take down that pesky Hitler. We already got him (at great cost), and you did nothing to help, asshole. Couldn't you at least refresh your bumper sticker with Kim Jong Un or Putin or ISIS or something? Man, you drive like an asshole.

Take it easy, Bro,

_____

Dear Asshole Who Hates
Saddam Hussein

TOURISTS AND FANS

Assholes Who Like to Look Around in Amazement While Driving

Dear Asshole Tour Guide
Showing His Relatives the Sights,

Everyone's very impressed that you know
about all the popular tourist destinations
in town. I'm sure your family loves
experiencing the same places they've seen
on TV firsthand, especially through the
unwashed windshield of your Honda Civic.
But what you can really do to enhance
their trip is to drive as slowly as you can
as you point and jabber on about the role
these "sights" play in your day-to-day life.

"Oh no way. You drive past this every day
on your way to work? You don't even notice
it anymore? Because the important `career`
that brought you here has ground you down
to a barely functioning husk of water and
flesh? Passively letting years pass by
until you inevitably move back home? How
interesting!" Out of the way, sad asshole.

High-five,

Dear Asshole Tour
Guide Showing His
Relatives the Sights

Dear Asshole Not Paying Attention to the Road,

You drive so well for someone who is blind. I mean REALLY well. Sure, you are swerving in and out of lanes, and your head is looking in the wrong direction and everything, but hey, you're blind, right? I can't even imagine the courage it must take to drive while blind. Of course, if you are not blind, then you are just a fucking mouth-breathing, moronic shithead who has no attention span, and you should be forced to eat your driver's license! You drive like an asshole!!

Outraged at your dumbfuckery,

_____

Dear Asshole Not Paying
Attention to the Road

DEAR COUNTRY-BUMPKIN ASSHOLE,

HYUCK, HYUCK! THE BIG CITY! GARSH! LOOKEE AT ALL THOSE BIG BUILDIN'S. EVERYTHING IS SO GARSH-DARN FAST! I JUST CAN'T KEEP UP. GARSH, GOLLY-GEE. AND ALL THEM-THAR FLASHIN' LIGHTS. I KIN HARDLY TELL THE RED LIGHTS FROM ALL THE OTHER BLINKIN' BIG-CITY LIGHTS. GARSH!

ALL RIGHT, CUT THE CRAP! I DON'T KNOW WHY THE FUCK YOU'RE HERE, BUT OBVIOUSLY YOU CAN DRIVE BECAUSE YOUR LICENSE PLATE INDICATES THAT YOU DROVE FROM SEVERAL MILLION LIGHT-YEARS AWAY. AND YOU PROBABLY STARTED DRIVING A FUCKING TRACTOR WHEN YOU WERE TEN MONTHS OLD. I KNOW BUILDIN'S AIN'T CORNFIELDS AND SUCH, BUT PLEASE STOP LOOKING AROUND IN AMAZEMENT—AND START DRIVING, ASSHOLE!

GO SIT ON A CORNHUSK,

_____

P.S. DON'T FORGET TO PULL IT BACK OUT.

DEAR COUNTRY-BUMPKIN ASSHOLE

Dear City-Slicker Asshole,

Don't you know that cars can't drive on a dirt road without getting at least a few scratches? Now you see why everyone drives pickups. Yes! These roads are made of billions of tiny rocks that will fly into the air and dent your precious car. Stop driving so slowly and gingerly, and just let your stupid car get scratched! For fuck's sake, that city you live in is a massive petri dish of human filth. Stop acting like the countryside is gross. You drive like an asshole!

Hope your car gets hit by a moose,

_____

Dear City-Slicker Asshole

Dear Asshole Driving the
Double-Decker Bus,

Never in my life have I been behind a bus
that drives so fucking slowly. Ooooh, it's a
double-decker. So what? I don't care. Will
the bus tip over if you take the turn too
fast? How do you know? Let's find out.
What? Double-decker buses aren't allowed to
tip over and crash? Nothing has a perfect
safety record, jerkface. You drive like a
double-decker asshole!

Unimpressed,

_____

Dear Asshole Driving
the Double-Decker Bus

Dear Asshole Driving the Bus Loaded with Asshole Senior Citizens,

I get it. You have a busload of old people, so you have gone insane. Are you taking them to eat the early-bird special at an oldies diner, or whatever the fuck they do out in Buttfuck, Egypt? At least take them somewhere with a huge parking lot so you don't have to clog up the road while dropping them off in Atlantic City, or wherever the fuck it is old people go.

Better yet, can't you just drive them around in circles, drop them back off, and tell them they had a good time? I promise they'll never know. You drive like an asshole.

Hope this helps,

_____

Dear Asshole Driving the Bus Loaded with Asshole Senior Citizens

Dear Tour-Guide Asshole with the Unsafe Van,

What the fuck are you driving? A van with the roof cut off? Who came up with that idea? What kind of tour is this? People actually pay you money? Hear ye, hear ye, the unsafe tour of shit is about to begin! Come sit in my structurally unsound, homemade, carnival shit van that will crush your head when it rolls over because I drive like an asshole!

Go live underground,

_____

Dear Tour-Guide Asshole
with the Unsafe Van

Dear Asshole on the Way
to the Pro-Wrestling Show,

Oh my God, you are on the way to pro wrestling, aren't you? Oh my God, they let you have children! Isn't there a law that forces you to be sterilized if you are an adult pro-wrestling fan? Wait, I get it. You are going because it's your kid's birthday. Maybe I was too harsh. Oh my God, there are no kids in your car! You're just two full-grown adults who are totally psyched to be going to pro wrestling! You must be in a hurry because you just have to see every match. Please slow down and stop driving like such an asshole.

Warmest nonregards,

_____

P.S. I hope wrestler sweat gets in your eyes and you blindly wander past the barrier and get hit with a steel chair.

Dear Asshole on the Way to the Pro-Wrestling Show

Dear Asshole on the Way to the Big Game,

Why are you honking and yelling, "WOOOO"!? Why is your face two colors? Is that a foam finger? You can't drive safely with a foam finger, yelling "WOOOO." Don't yell "WOOOO" on the way to the game. Yell "WOOOO" at the game, you moron. That's why they have huge stadiums—for you to act like a jackass in them. You can even act like a fuckhead in the parking lot. I hope your face stays that color and your foam finger gets cancer. You drive like an asshole.

Here's hoping your team loses,

_____

Dear Asshole on the
Way to the Big Game

Dear Asshole on the Way to a Rave,

What is wrong with all of you? Can't you just join the circus, or something? There aren't enough drugs in the world to make me want to go where you are going. How many of you are packed into that car? You do realize that EDM is unlistenable if you are not stoned out of your mind, don't you? How old are you? You can't even see over the steering wheel, and you're driving around in some weird warehouse district. Maybe you could park in that barn where the guy with the overalls wearing the hockey mask and carrying the axe is standing. You drive like an asshole.

See ya in the next life,

_____

Dear Asshole on the
Way to a Rave

EVERYDAY ASSHOLES

Dear Minivan-Soccer-Mom Asshole,

Clearly you've gone insane from all the screaming kids in your minivan. I'm sure you have ice cream in the back of your hair and you can't distinguish the honking horns from the white noise of your idiot kids. I'm sure even a fighter pilot would be impressed by your multitasking skills. Perhaps you could put your kids in a trailer behind the car. Or send them to boarding school. Or get a divorce and send them off to live with their father. Or glue fur on them and take them to the pound. Something! Because you are driving like an asshole!

With appreciation,

_____

Dear Minivan-Soccer-
Mom Asshole

Dear Smiling Asshole with the Chihuahuas on Her Lap,

How adorable—you're out for a ride with your dogs. Oh, I just wanted to inform you: This isn't a parade where people are lined up to look at you. This is real life. Stop driving with your dogs hanging out the window while you hope people will notice you. Nobody cares. We've all seen Chihuahuas before, and we all know how annoying they are. I hope your dogs get diarrhea and shit all over your lap. You drive like an asshole.

Woof, woof, shut that yapping hamster up,

Dear Smiling Asshole with
the Chihuahuas on Her Lap

Dear Asshole Looking at an Actual Paper Map,

Are you really looking at a paper map? What?! What year is this?! We have robots that tell you where to go now, like not even the crappy robots in the movies that talk all slow and shit and make weird calculating sounds. There are real robots that talk to satellites in space and tell you how to get somewhere. Oh, I'm sorry. Is using a GPS system too confusing for you? I'm sure operating a vehicle capable of obliterating a small crowd of people is within your grasp. Here, have a state-issued license that gives you the right to do so!

Look at you fumble with that paper map with your sepia-toned hands. I'm sure you smell like couch farts. You know, the decades of farts you've been farting into the cushions of your couch while you adjust your spectacles so you can see your tube-powered television? Yeah, those. Yeeeeesh! You drive like an old-timey asshole.

With empathy,

_____

P.S. Welcome to the future, asshole.

Dear Asshole Looking at
an Actual Paper Map

Dear Asshole with the Perpetually on Blinker,

TURN YOUR BLINKER OFF. You're crippling every driver around you with your oblivious bullshit. Look, I get that you're either old or stoned, but in either case, why don't you actually use that blinker to get off the highway and go to a park or something. You could feed birds or play chess with a homeless man or just sit in the sun. Doesn't that sound nice? Nicer than what you're currently doing, which is the equivalent of screaming "I'M GOING TO HIT YOU" in someone's face over and over again, and then never actually doing it. Doesn't that sound like the worst psychological prison? Like a thousand terrorist threats with no specific target. Get off the road, asshole.

Signed,

_____

Dear Asshole with the
Perpetually on Blinker

Dear Asshole Who Refuses to Merge,

Fuck! Merge already! MERGE! MERGE! Are you unmergeable? Are you waiting for road to run out? If you were an airline pilot, would you simply never pull up and run the plane right off the runway?

MERGE!!! I'm yelling the word "merge" so many times at you that I am becoming aware of how weird the word sounds. Now I'm starting to yell other phrases:

"Blend in!" "Amalgam!" "Will you please fucking commingle with the rest of us?" MEEEEEEERGE! You are driving like an asshole!

Yours in the blissful union of merge,

_____

Dear Asshole Who
Refuses to Merge

Dear Overly Friendly Asshole Who Lets Everyone Merge in Front of Her,

I'm sorry your dad was an asshole. I'm sorry he never listened to you or allowed you to speak up. That must have really, really sucked. But you're not pleasing him by letting everyone walk all over you. Nothing will make you feel like you've done enough for him until you realize he could never have been pleased in the first place. In fact, you could let the entire fucking lane cut ahead of you, but it still wouldn't transform the past.

Look at yourself. Take a long, hard look. You're a good person. You have value. Stand up straight, push those shoulders back, firm up that handshake, and then TAKE YOUR OWN TURN, asshole. Stop being a meek, passive asshole, and instead be a strong, assertive asshole. Now's the time. You can do it, asshole.

Empoweringly yours,

———————————

P.S. #DaddyIssues

Dear Overly Friendly Asshole
Who Lets Everyone Merge
in Front of Her

Dear Asshole Who Turns Left
with the Right Blinker on,

It's one thing to forget you have your blinker
on. That just makes you a regular moron. It's
happened to all of us, I'm sure. But when you
turn in the opposite direction of where your
blinker says you are going to turn, well, that
makes you a whole other level of moron—a
mega-moron, if you will. If you ignore your
blinker all the time, then how did it get on in
the first place? Do you have multiple driving
personalities? Are you trying to shake a
tail? I want a cop to pull you over. I am not
vindictive. I don't want you to get a ticket,
but I do think you should have to give a
response to the following question: What the
fuck is wrong with you? You sure do drive
like an asshole.

Puzzled,

_____

Dear Asshole Who Turns Left
with the Right Blinker on

Dear Asshole Who Won't Drive over 25 MPH,

Ever feel like a rotten tree trunk in the middle of a raging river? Because that is what you are—a rat-and-maggot-infested, rotten tree trunk in the middle of a raging river. We normal motorists are the water surging around you as you sit there and rot. You can't even save the filthy rats and disgusting maggots that ingest you. You just slowly rot as everything rushes past you. You are in slow motion. You are slow-witted. You drag ass, and you suck. Why don't you just get a motorized wheelchair? It would be cheaper for you, and you could go to dumb fuck camp with the savings. You drive like an asshole.

Poetically,

_____

Dear Asshole Who Won't
Drive over 25 MPH

Dear Asshole with the Bass-Thumping Super Woofer,

Excuse me! Something is dribbling from your ears. Could it be your brains? Are they turning to Jell-O? This huge, low-frequency thumping has to affect other parts of you, too. I'll bet your teeth are loose and you are currently shitting your pants. Could you do me a favor? Could you drive around with someone who knows sign language? That way they could read people's lips and relay to you all the things people are yelling at you on the road. Better yet, could you drive into a building or a ditch? If I heard that super bass coming out of a car on fire, well, that would make my day. You drive like an asshole.

Fondly,

_____

P.S. SHUT THAT THING OFF!

Dear Asshole with the Bass-Thumping Super Woofer

Dear Asshole Listening to Earbuds While Driving,

I'm not sure it is wise to take away your sense of hearing when you drive. Why don't you put a blindfold on? That would actually be safer. You would still be able to hear a horn honk, and you could still slam on the brakes. I hope you are listening to some motivational speaker. I hope you get an epiphany and come up with a million-dollar idea moments before you are hit by a train. You drive like an asshole.

Awaiting your demise,

_____

Dear Asshole Listening
to Earbuds While Driving

Dear Asshole with the Driver's Seat Pushed All the Way into the Backseat,

What the fuck is this? I know it's called the "gangsta lean" or the "cugine lean" or whatever. I guess maybe it makes it harder to get shot or something? Meanwhile, most bullets I know go through doors. Also, most assassins I know won't think it is a magical, driverless car. They will still shoot into the area known as the "driver's seat," but I digress.

Look, I don't care if you drive with your genitals and your ass hanging out the window, as long as your asshole has a working eyeball in it! When you're lying down, though, YOU CAN'T SEE WHERE THE FUCK YOU ARE GOING! That's, like, one of the top things you need to do when driving!! It's a shitty car, by the way. And with all due respect, you drive like an asshole.

Later,

_____

Dear Asshole with the
Driver's Seat Pushed All
the Way into the Backseat

DEAR ASSHOLE DRIVING IN THE CARPOOL LANE,

I PRIDE MYSELF ON BEING AN INCLUSIVE PERSON. I TRY TO BE OPEN-MINDED AND ADAPTABLE. I ABHOR DISCRIMINATION OF ALL KINDS. I'D LIKE TO THINK IF I HAD BEEN AROUND IN THE MIDST OF THE CIVIL RIGHTS MOVEMENT, I WOULD HAVE BEEN AMONG THE BRAVE PROTESTERS MARCHING ON SELMA, NOT ONE OF THE BIGOTS CLINGING TO SEGREGATION.

BUT THIS LANE, THIS CARPOOL LANE, IS LIKE A LITTLE CLUB HERE. IT'S AN EXCLUSIVE AND PRIVILEGED CLUB, AND YOU'RE NOT ALLOWED IN IT. NOT BECAUSE OF YOUR RACE, AGE, OR SEX, BUT RATHER BECAUSE—HMMM, HOW DO I PUT THIS DELICATELY?—THE CARPOOL LANE IS LIKE A CLUB FOR PEOPLE WITH FRIENDS, AND, BY ALL INDICATIONS, YOU DO NOT HAVE ANY FRIENDS. AND THEREFORE, YOU ARE NOT ALLOWED IN OUR CARPOOL CLUB.

THOSE OF US IN THE CARPOOL CLUB HAVE WORKED OUR ENTIRE LIVES TO CULTIVATE AND NURTURE MEANINGFUL FRIENDSHIPS WITH OTHER PEOPLE. WE HAVE FOUGHT HARD TO MAKE OURSELVES LOVABLE AND LOVED, TO EARN THAT COMPANION IN OUR PASSENGER SEATS. YOU, A CRETIN WITHOUT A COMPANION, ARE NOT ENTITLED TO THE SAME PERKS AS US: THE FRIENDLY, THE LOVED, THE WANTED. PLEASE GO BACK TO THE LONELY SECTION OF THE HIGHWAY WITH THE OTHER LONELY HEARTS ENCASED IN THEIR METAL TOMBS OF SOLITUDE. YOU DRIVE LIKE A LONELY ASSHOLE.

XOXO,

_____

P.S. PERHAPS YOU COULD GET A BLOW-UP DOLL. THEN MAYBE WE'D ALLOW YOUR KIND INTO OUR CLUB.

DEAR ASSHOLE DRIVING IN
THE CARPOOL LANE

Dear Asshole Student Driver,

This is truly a special moment. I'm watching an asshole being born. You are like a baby shark loaded with teeth and raring to go—a perfect creature of asshole evolution. You don't even need to learn how to drive like an asshole. You're doing it immediately! It's breathtaking. Isn't nature wonderful? Perhaps one day you will become one of the rare majestic creatures who learns not to drive like an asshole, but that is a long shot. Until then, you drive like an asshole.

Welcome to the motoring public,

_____

P.S. See the driving instructor next to you? See how impressed he is by your ability to scare the fuck out of him? See how he constantly flinches and blinks? You have driven him insane.

Dear Asshole
Student Driver